ASTEROIDS
in the Bible?

HENRY W. WRIGHT

HENRY W. WRIGHT

Be in Health
4178 Crest Highway
Thomaston, Georgia 30286

www.beinhealth.com

EAN: 978-1-934680-23-0

Copyright Notice

© Copyright: 2009. Be in Health™

All rights reserved. Any material, be it in written form, audio, video, compact disc, website postings – whether it be text, HTML, audio streaming or graphic images related to Be in Health™ may not be mirrored, reproduced, or displayed in whole or in part on another webpage or website (whatever the nature or purpose), or in any publication or collection of widespread circulation, whether offline or online (whatever the nature or purpose), even if considered "fair use," without express written permission from Be in Health™.

Disclaimer

This ministry does not seek to be in conflict with any medical or psychiatric practices nor do we seek to be in conflict with any church and its religious doctrines, beliefs or practices. We are not a part of medicine or psychology, yet we work to make them more effective, rather than working against them. We believe many human problems are fundamentally spiritual with associated physiological and psychological manifestations. This information is intended for your general knowledge only. Information is presented only to give insight into disease, its problems and its possible solutions in the area of disease eradication and/or prevention. It is not a substitute for medical advice or treatment for specific medical conditions or disorders. You should seek prompt medical care for any specific health issues. Treatment modalities around your specific health issues are between you and your physician.

As pastors, ministers, and individuals of this ministry, we are not responsible for a person's disease, nor are we responsible for his/her healing. All we can do is share what we see about a problem. We are not professionals; we are not healers. We are only ministers administering the Scriptures, and what they say about this subject, along with what the medical and scientific communities have also observed in line with this insight. There is no guarantee that any person will be healed or any disease be prevented. The fruits of this teaching will come forth out of the relationship between the person and God based on these insights given and applied. This ministry is patterned after the following scriptures: 2 Corinthians 5:18-20; 1 Corinthians 12; Ephesians 4; Mark 16:15-20.

Preface

This booklet was developed from a teaching to a live audience and has been kept in a conversational format. It is designed to reach a personal level with the reader rather than present a structured, theological presentation. Many times the reader will feel Henry Wright is talking directly to him/her. The frequent use of the pronoun "you" is meant to penetrate the human heart.

Table of Contents

News Articles about Asteroids 1

Astronomer's Report (2002 NT7) 7

Prophetic Timeline 9

Myth about the Tribulation 19

Myth – The Elect will be here 21

The Bible and Asteroids 23

Prophecy Fulfilled 25

Tribulation Period 31

The First Trumpet 37

The Second Trumpet 39

The Third Trumpet 41

The Fourth Trumpet 45

The Fifth Trumpet 47

The Sixth Trumpet 49

The Seventh Trumpet 53

    Prayer 55

    Bibliography 57

> **The first angel sounded, and there followed hail and fire mingled with blood, and they were cast upon the earth: and the third part of trees was burnt up, and all green grass was burnt up.**
>
> Revelation 8:7

ASTEROIDS
in the Bible?

The news is filled with the big question: "Will planet earth ever be hit by a gigantic asteroid?" People are thinking about it and that makes it current events. We need to be able to understand what is happening in our generation in terms of the Bible. It is of eternal significance.

NEWS ARTICLES ABOUT ASTEROIDS

US News and World Report, January 15, 2001, has a picture of a large stone asteroid in space and the article is called "Heading Our Way."

In *Discover Magazine,* February 2001, there is a front-page article called "Rendezvous with a Killer Asteroid" concerning what is in space and will an asteroid hit our planet?

Newsweek Magazine, talks about the close calls of space junk and space rock. An article called "The Science of Doom," dated November 23, 1992, says space is filled with objects that threaten earth. Researchers are scrambling to insure that worlds do not collide.

"Strange Space Object Heads Toward Earth" is the title of an article from several years ago in the *Florida Times-Union, November 20, 1991,* about an asteroid that flew within 106,000 miles of the earth on January 15, 1991. It was orbiting the sun at about 69,000 miles per hour and closing in on the earth at 2,900 miles per hour.

There are asteroids of all sizes out there, but one of the big ones is about the size of one of the small islands of Hawaii—14 miles long and 9 miles wide.

The *Atlanta Journal-Constitution*, February 17, 1997, ran an article called "The Smoking Gun." The smoking gun is residue from a world that existed long before Adam. Scientists have drilled about 300 miles down into the sea and brought up sediment. Buried on top of that was residue of material that can only come from an asteroid. The material is not common to this planet and it involves the chemical iridium. It covered what was life that existed here on planet earth that was later destroyed.

There are those who believe the earth had its beginning with Adam and Eve only 6000 years ago. Yet asteroids hit this planet long before Adam and Eve. There is also a lot of conversation about the Ice Age and the Bible is very clear in Jeremiah 4:15-24 that civilization on this planet was destroyed in the eternal past. All fruitful places, all of mankind and all the cities in their entirety were destroyed.

Verses 15-22 is the judgment and verses 23-24 is the result of that judgment.

> **[15]For a voice declareth from Dan, and publisheth affliction from mount Ephraim.**

> [16]Make ye mention to the nations; behold, publish against Jerusalem, that watchers come from a far country, and give out their voice against the cities of Judah.
>
> [17]As keepers of a field, are they against her round about; because she hath been rebellious against me, saith the LORD.
>
> [18]Thy way and thy doings have procured these things unto thee; this is thy wickedness, because it is bitter, because it reacheth unto thine heart.
>
> [19]My bowels, my bowels! I am pained at my very heart; my heart maketh a noise in me; I cannot hold my peace, because thou hast heard, O my soul, the sound of the trumpet, the alarm of war.
>
> [20]Destruction upon destruction is cried; for the whole land is spoiled: suddenly are my tents spoiled, and my curtains in a moment.
>
> [21]How long shall I see the standard, and hear the sound of the trumpet?
>
> [22]For my people is foolish, they have not known me; they are sottish children, and they have none understanding: they are wise to do evil, but to do good they have no knowledge.
>
> [23]I beheld the earth, and, lo, it was without form, and void; and the heavens, and they had no light.
>
> [24]I beheld the mountains, and, lo, they trembled, and all the hills moved lightly. Jeremiah 4:15-24

This matches Genesis 1:2, which says the earth was without form and void and darkness was upon the face of the deep.

> And the earth was without form, and void; and darkness *was* upon the face of the deep. And the Spirit of God moved upon the face of the waters.
> Genesis 1:2

If you do a lot of reading, you have seen there is much speculation. *USA Today*, February 23, 2001, features the article, "A Comet May Have Triggered Mass Extinction." That includes the dinosaurs and everything that existed at one time.

Another story in the *National Geographic News*, which is dated April 9, 2002, is about a large asteroid headed for impact with the earth in 2880.

In a *Florida Times-Union* article, astronomers wonder when the big one will hit. They say the earth is bound to be hit; it is a statistical certainty. It is unlikely that a really large asteroid will hit in our lifetime, but it is not beyond the pale. Statistically, though, the risk of death from an asteroid is higher per person than dying in an airplane crash.

This asteroid, or what they call a "doomsday rock," if it were large enough, would severely disrupt life on earth upon impact, lofting pulverized rock and dust that would block most sunlight. Agriculture would virtually end and civilization could wither and die. These are speculations.

I read another article that said one missed us by 106,000 miles! If it had struck the earth, it would have caused a disaster unprecedented in human history. The energy released would have been equivalent to more than 1000 one-megaton bombs. That is pretty powerful!

"Scientists gathered together today to make plans on how to divert killer asteroids" according to an article in the *Florida Times-Union*, July 1, 1991. According to scientists, to develop the technology to divert it will take 20 more years after it has already hit. So the technology to send out rockets to blast these things and move them out of their course is not even here today! According to my research, the technology to be able to intercept a large asteroid, blast it and divert it, is about 40 years out.

We are talking about widespread destruction, with half of the earth's people starving after the planet's climate and farming are destroyed by the impact of the mile-wide asteroid. Several asteroids will pass within 10 million miles of earth this year alone.

The *Times-Union* says the closest call came when that 30-foot wide asteroid swept within 106,000 miles. "Growing evidence suggests a 6-mile wide asteroid whacked the earth 65 million years ago, killing 2/3 of all species, including dinosaurs. Somewhat smaller, doomsday rocks, asteroids wider than one mile, strike the planet once every 300,000 to 1 million years. That frequency means any individual's risk of dying in a big impact is 1 in 6,000 to 1 in 20,000 during the next 50 years."

The risk that it will say on your tombstone, "Killed as a result of an asteroid impact" is somewhat greater than chances you will be killed in an airplane crash and much greater than being killed by fireworks, tornadoes, volcanic eruptions, nuclear accidents or terrorism. Statistically, the chances of being killed on this planet by an asteroid outdistance all of the above things you are currently afraid of!

Astronomer's Report (2002 NT7)

Scientists say the earth is a sitting duck in a cosmic shooting gallery of asteroids. From *CNN*, July 24, 2002, "Astronomers are carefully monitoring a newly discovered 1.2 mile wide asteroid to see if it is on a collision course with earth." This is a big one. One and two-tenths miles across, it is an asteroid capable of doing incredible damage if it hits this planet.

"Initial calculations indicate there is a chance the asteroid known as 2002 NT7 will hit the earth on February 1, 2019. This is the one they are now watching, and it is on a direct collision course with this planet. The expected landing date is not very far away!

Some say, "It may never happen."

Well, it may happen! And I'm going to show you from scriptures that this planet will be hit, not by 1, not by 2, but by 3 asteroids within a 3½ year period. There should be awareness that time is short: not from a fear standpoint, but from a salvation standpoint. It is time to wake up and not be lulled into the ongoing things of life as if God will not pull a plug on time in the near future!

Reuters says a massive asteroid could hit the earth in just a few years' time, destroying life as we know it. It is 1.2 miles wide and apparently on a direct collision course with earth. In the worst-case scenario, a disaster this size would be global in its extent. It would create a meltdown of our economic and social life and would reduce us to Dark Ages conditions.

The calculations show it could hit the earth on February 1, 2019. This is the first asteroid that has been given a rating of "1" in the history of asteroid observation and that rating means the chances of it hitting are 1 in 1. There's not much chance that it isn't going to happen!

The article from *Reuters* states, "Sooner or later—and no one can really tell us which it will be—we will find an object that is on a collision course and eventually we will have to deflect an object from its collision course."

That is as certain as "Amen" in the church!

The article further states that, at the moment, scientists fear it would take at least 30 years for the world to be able to devise and set up a mission to deal with such a threat. This is a time scale which would woefully be inadequate if the 2019 strike were to happen.

"Last month an asteroid the size of a soccer field missed the earth by 75,000 miles, less than 1/3 of the distance to the moon," states an article in the *Associated Press* dated July 24, 2002. "Scientists said if it had hit a populated area, it would have released as much energy as a large nuclear weapon."

Since these articles are in the news, what do you do with these subjects as a believer? Let's see what the Bible says about this topic so we can approach the subject with some type of intelligence and knowledge rather than falling into a type of morbidity and fear.

Prophetic Timeline

The church is in major confusion about prophetic timeline. There are those who teach about the tribulation period. There are those who teach about the Millennium that follows the tribulation period. There are those in Christianity who teach there is no such thing as the Millennium.

One notable Christian organization in the world does not believe in the thousand-year reign of Christ and teaches against the Millennium. Some organizations teach there is no such thing as the second coming of Christ. They teach He has come already in the church.

That cannot be true because the church is in confusion. There are those who do not believe in the tribulation period. There are those who believe we are in the tribulation period now.

There are those who teach we are in the Millennium now. There are the pre-tribbers. They believe the rapture comes before the tribulation. That is the first resurrection in Scripture. It would be the equivalent, but the word "rapture" is not found in Scripture. Instead, the Bible says, "Blessed are they that have part in the first resurrection, for they shall not taste of the second death."

> **Blessed and holy *is* he that hath part in the first resurrection: on such the second death hath no power, but they shall be priests of God and of Christ, and shall reign with him a thousand years.** Revelation 20:6

What is the second death? Being cast alive into the lake of fire at the white throne judgment.

> And death and hell were cast into the lake of fire.
> This is the second death. Revelation 20:14

Blessed are they who have part in the first resurrection, for they shall not taste of the second death. This means if you are part of the first resurrection, you go to the judgment seat of Christ.

> But why dost thou judge thy brother? or why dost thou set at nought thy brother? for we shall all stand before the judgment seat of Christ. Romans 14:10

> For we must all appear before the judgment seat of Christ; that every one may receive the things *done* in *his* body, according to that he hath done, whether *it be* good or bad. 2 Corinthians 5:10

If you miss the first resurrection, you go to the white throne judgment to give an answer to God the Father as to why you rejected the gospel message.

> [11]And I saw a great white throne, and him that sat on it, from whose face the earth and the heaven fled away; and there was found no place for them.
>
> [12]And I saw the dead, small and great, stand before God; and the books were opened: and another book was opened, which is *the book* of life: and the dead were judged out of those things which were written in the books, according to their works.
>
> [13]And the sea gave up the dead which were in it; and death and hell delivered up the dead which were in them: and they were judged every man according to their works. Revelation 20:11-13

Every man from Adam who has lived or died in covenant, or in rebellion against covenant, will stand before either the Lord Jesus Christ or Father God to give an account for his deeds—good or evil. In the resurrection of the damned, he will stand before the

Father in the white throne judgment. In the resurrection of the believers, he shall stand eventually before Jesus in heaven in something called the judgment seat of Christ.

There are those who believe the church will be taken out of this mess *before* the tribulation; these are pre-tribbers. Then you have those who say the church will be taken out in the *middle* of the tribulation; those are mid-tribbers. Then there are those who say the church will be here *through* the tribulation; those are post-tribbers. And then you have those who say there is no tribulation and those are no-tribbers.

Pre-trib, mid-trib, post-trib, no trib, whatever; do not miss it! Do not miss your destiny. It is your God-given right to read the Bible and find your own position. Besides, what will happen to you in the future is not worth debating about. The method is not worth debating about. You first must be born again! That is the only issue.

According to Scripture, the antichrist, the false messiah, is revealed during the tribulation period. The nation of Israel accepts this false messiah as the true Messiah and he offers himself to them and they accept him and worship him. Then in the middle of this 7-year period (3½ years into it), they come to synagogue one Sabbath and instead of seeing their beloved messiah they have been worshipping for 3½ years, they find his image as a statue in the holy of holies in the new temple. This is the temple Israel will be building in the future.

> And he shall confirm the covenant with many for one week: and in the midst of the week he shall cause the sacrifice and the oblation to cease, and for the overspreading of abominations he shall make *it* desolate, even until the consummation, and that determined shall be poured upon the desolate.
>
> Daniel 9:27

First of all, it is an abomination to bow your knee and worship a graven image.

> ³Thou shalt have no other gods before me.
>
> ⁴Thou shalt not make unto thee any graven image, or any likeness *of any thing* that *is* in heaven above, or that *is* in the earth beneath, or that *is* in the water under the earth:
>
> ⁵Thou shalt not bow down thyself to them, nor serve them: for I the LORD thy God *am* a jealous God, visiting the iniquity of the fathers upon the children unto the third and fourth *generation* of them that hate me;
>
> Exodus 20:3-5

The desolation is that when they refuse to bow the knee, their beloved messiah turns on them in a holocaust that will make what happened in Germany look like a tea party. And for 3½ years, there is nothing but horrible hell on this planet. It is going to be a mess. We will show you just how destructive the affairs on this planet will be and we will narrow it down to a 3½-year period and then you will see where the asteroids come in.

It is my opinion and my position that the first resurrection occurs before the revelation of the antichrist. Mine is the position of a pre-tribber. The chronological sequence of the book of Revelation shows us it is impossible to believe the church will be here on the earth in the tribulation period.

The first resurrection takes place in the great chaos coming out of the fulfillment of Ezekiel 38 and 39. This is explained in detail in our tape series called "Prophetic Timeline." It deals with what is happening in Israel today, what will happen in the future and what is going to happen next on this planet.

In the chaos of that timing, the first resurrection occurs. When the first resurrection occurs, the time of the Gentiles is finished.

Someone recently said, "Well, if I just didn't get right with God and I wasn't part of the first resurrection, but I love God, on that very next day, or that very next week after the first resurrection, I can get right with God. I have a second chance. I know I've missed it, but I love God so I'm going to tell Him I love Him and He's going to accept me."

That is faulty thinking. If you are not a Jew, it is over with because the time of the Gentiles is finished. During the tribulation period, the 7 years (3½ years of peace and 3½ years of horror), God centers His attention only on national Israel in order to give national Israel one more chance to bow their knee to Him.

When you study what is going to happen in those years, the gospel is preached from the heavens even by angels to those on the earth (the natural Jews) so that they may repent. The two witnesses are in Jerusalem for three years and they confront the antichrist. People try to kill the two witnesses, but they are unable to do so.

The two witnesses confront and teach and preach and finally they are killed. Their bodies lie in the streets of Jerusalem for 3½ days, stinking, and then God raises them from the dead and they stand up as a thrust in the face of Satan.

> ³And I will give *power* unto my two witnesses, and they shall prophesy a thousand two hundred and threescore days, clothed in sackcloth.
>
> ⁵And if any man will hurt them, fire proceedeth out of their mouth, and devoureth their enemies: and if any man will hurt them, he must in this manner be killed.
>
> ⁷And when they shall have finished their testimony, the beast that ascendeth out of the bottomless pit shall make war against them, and shall overcome them, and kill them.
>
> ⁹And they of the people and kindreds and tongues and nations shall see their dead bodies three days and an half, and shall not suffer their dead bodies to be put in graves.
>
> ¹¹And after three days and an half the Spirit of life from God entered into them, and they stood upon their feet; and great fear fell upon them which saw them. Revelation 11:3,5,7,9,11

Who are the two witnesses? We teach they are Moses and Elijah. Many teach it is Enoch, yet Enoch was in a prior time, in a world that was judged by the flood. He has nothing more to say, but Elijah does.

Now I want to tell you about Moses. God raised him from the dead because you see him appearing in the mount of transfiguration with Jesus and Elijah.

> ³And, behold, there appeared unto them Moses and Elias talking with him.
>
> ⁴Then answered Peter, and said unto Jesus, Lord, it is good for us to be here: if thou wilt, let us make here three tabernacles; one for thee, and one for Moses, and one for Elias.　　　　　　　　　Matthew 17:3-4

Many are concerned about the antichrist now. There are books and tapes out which indicate the antichrist will control this whole world. Everyone is concerned about the mark of the beast. In the first resurrection, according to Scripture, in the cycles of Daniel's 69 weeks, there is a 7-year period fulfilled at the end of this age and those 7 years are the tribulation period on the earth. So the church will not have to worry about the mark of the beast because the church will be in heaven.

In heaven, there are two things happening: the judgment seat of Christ and the marriage supper of the Lamb.

> **For we must all appear before the judgment seat of Christ; that every one may receive the things** *done* **in** *his* **body, according to that he hath done, whether** *it be* **good or bad.**　　　　　　　　2 Corinthians 5:10
>
> **And he saith unto me, Write, Blessed** *are* **they which are called unto the marriage supper of the Lamb. And he saith unto me, These are the true sayings of God.**　　　　　　　　Revelation 19:9

And then in Zechariah 14:1-5, with the LORD at the lead and all the saints with Him, the church comes back to confront the antichrist and his hordes in the valley of Megiddo. That will be the end of that mess and the beginning of the 45 days of cleansing, according to

Daniel in the setting up of the millennial kingdom. This begins the thousand-year reign of Christ and the saints.

> ¹**Behold, the day of the LORD cometh, and thy spoil shall be divided in the midst of thee.**
>
> ²**For I will gather all nations against Jerusalem to battle; and the city shall be taken, and the houses rifled, and the women ravished; and half of the city shall go forth into captivity, and the residue of the people shall not be cut off from the city.**
>
> ³**Then shall the LORD go forth, and fight against those nations, as when he fought in the day of battle.**
>
> ⁴**And his feet shall stand in that day upon the mount of Olives, which is before Jerusalem on the east, and the mount of Olives shall cleave in the midst thereof toward the east and toward the west, and there shall be a very great valley; and half of the mountain shall remove toward the north, and half of it toward the south.**
>
> ⁵**And ye shall flee to the valley of the mountains; for the valley of the mountains shall reach unto Azal: yea, ye shall flee, like as ye fled from before the earthquake in the days of Uzziah king of Judah: and the LORD my God shall come,** *and* **all the saints with thee.**   Zechariah 14:1-5

The timeline is very simple. The antichrist does not rule the whole world. When you study his territories, he only rules 1 nation very strongly, 2 close confederates very strongly and 7 loosely.

But in the last 3½ years of tribulation that great holocaust is going on and the antichrist tries to exterminate the Jews and destroy Israel and Jerusalem once and for all. Then the king of the north and the king of the south come up and declare war on him.

If he controlled the whole planet, there is no way two great nations would even be there to declare war on him. So he has some problems to complicate his life near the end of those 3½ years before the Lord comes with the saints to deal with him.

Myth about the Tribulation

There is a myth that the church will be here in the tribulation, but immune to the judgments. If an asteroid hits here today, it will not be just the unbelievers who die. There are those who think they are immune and will be living in communes somewhere, hidden away in the rocks in survival mentality.

There is a mentality that God's people will be in the tribulation and are somehow protected. There is not one Scripture to prove that! The church is not here to be protected. *The church will not be here.* The ones who are here will be looking for the rocks to hide them.

> [15]And the kings of the earth, and the great men, and the rich men, and the chief captains, and the mighty men, and every bondman, and every free man, hid themselves in the dens and in the rocks of the mountains;
>
> [16]And said to the mountains and rocks, Fall on us, and hide us from the face of him that sitteth on the throne, and from the wrath of the Lamb:
> Revelation 6:15-16

Myth — The Elect will be here

The next myth in Christianity is that the elect of the church will be here living in bombproof shelters or hidden in forests living a survival existence until it is finished and then they pop out and turn the planet over as a gift. That also is not scriptural.

There are those teaching that the church will become so strong and so powerful that it will subdue this entire planet in righteousness and turn the planet over as a gift to Jesus. Then He will return.

Read Zechariah chapter 14. It says when the LORD comes, the planet has rebels on it. In fact, the land of Egypt refuses for three years to come up and bow their knee to the King in Jerusalem until they are smitten with famine to break their rebellion.

> **16And it shall come to pass, *that* every one that is left of all the nations which came against Jerusalem shall even go up from year to year to worship the King, the LORD of hosts, and to keep the feast of tabernacles.**
>
> **17And it shall be, that whoso will not come up of all the families of the earth unto Jerusalem to worship the King, the LORD of hosts, even upon them shall be no rain.**
>
> **18And if the family of Egypt go not up, and come not, that *have* no *rain*; there shall be the plague, wherewith the LORD will smite the heathen that come not up to keep the feast of tabernacles.**

> ¹⁹**This shall be the punishment of Egypt, and the punishment of all nations that come not up to keep the feast of tabernacles.** Zechariah 14:16-19

That does not mean the whole planet has been subdued in righteousness. The Bible teaches that a sinner who dies at 100 in the Millennium is cursed. This means there will be sinners.

> **There shall be no more thence an infant of days, nor an old man that hath not filled his days: for the child shall die an hundred years old; but the sinner** *being* **an hundred years old shall be accursed.**
> Isaiah 65:20

These theologies bouncing around are designed to give a superior, elitist mentality, so don't follow them!

THE BIBLE AND ASTEROIDS

What does the Bible say about asteroids? First of all, we are discussing this because it is found in the Bible, not just in newspaper headlines. Amos 3:7 says, "Surely the Lord GOD will do nothing, but he revealeth his secret unto his servants the prophets."

If you will notice the Lord GOD revelation here, this is not Jehovah Elohim, this is Adonai Jehovih. "Surely the Lord GOD (this is the Father), will do nothing, but He revealeth His secret unto His servants the prophets." "The lion hath roared, who will not fear? the Lord GOD hath spoken, but who can prophesy?"

> **7Surely the Lord GOD will do nothing, but he revealeth his secret unto his servants the prophets.**
>
> **8The lion hath roared, who will not fear? the Lord GOD hath spoken, who can but prophesy?** Amos 3:7-8

One of the things I love about God in prophetic timeline is: everything God has ever done, He first has prophesied it through some man. He has first, by the Spirit of God, established it through His prophets, right down to the coming of the Lord Jesus Christ, born of a virgin, dying for our sins.

Jesus himself fulfilled 337 direct prophecies from the Old Testament when He came.

Prophecy Fulfilled

Statisticians have told me that in terms of 6000 years (or at that time when He came, 4000 years), one man specifically fulfilling just one prophecy would be the equivalent of laying down quarters in the state of Texas, marking one with a red marker, then blindfolding an individual, sending them into the state of Texas and the first time they bent over they would pick up the red-marked quarter.

The chances for two prophecies being specifically fulfilled by one man in one generation in one time is the equivalent of this: Taking the moon, duplicating it in its diameter between the moon and earth, covering each moon with quarters, putting one marked red quarter on one of those moons and sending a blindfolded man to pick up that quarter. The statistical probability of one man fulfilling just *two* prophecies is the same as the blindfolded man picking up that red-marked quarter on the first moon, first try.

Jesus directly fulfilled 337 prophecies by the prophets. That gives us a good reason to follow Him. There is no need to be worrying about what Nostradamus has said, but there is a need to consider what the prophets have said. By understanding prophecy, you as a believer will know exactly what will be happening here in the next few years so that you are not deceived and you are not in fear. You can teach men the error of their ways so they can prepare their hearts to meet a living God.

Someone said the other day, "I don't read Revelation." There are Christian churches today who tell their people to disregard Revelation because it is so confusing they would never understand it anyway. They say, "Besides, it is a book of woes. You are believers and God is going to spare you, so you do not need to read it."

> **Blessed *is* he that readeth, and they that hear the words of this prophecy, and keep those things which are written therein: for the time *is* at hand.**
> Revelation 1:3

Blessed is he that readeth what? The words of the book of Revelation. Blessed is he that readeth and they that hear the words of this prophecy and keep those things which are written: for the time is at hand. It has been 2000 years. Remember, 1000 years is as 1 day with the Lord.

> **But, beloved, be not ignorant of this one thing, that one day *is* with the Lord as a thousand years, and a thousand years as one day.** 2 Peter 3:8

In God's timing, He has been hanging around only a couple of days!

Now here is a chronology of prophetic timeline that pinpoints when the asteroids are coming. First of all, Revelation 5 shows a scene in heaven. Revelation 1 is the introduction to the book. Revelation 2 and 3 are the addresses to seven New Testament churches and their spiritual conditions. Those seven churches are indicative of seven specific churches and their spirituality.

Revelation 2 and 3 are indicative of seven spiritual characteristics of the Christian church age. It is also indicative of seven divisions of time of the New Testament church. Today, we find ourselves a member of one or two of those churches spiritually: the church at Laodicea or the church at Philadelphia. It would be good if we were members of the church of Philadelphia in the metaphorical sense, because Jesus found nothing wrong with it. To the church at Laodicea, He said, "I will spew you out of my mouth."

> **So then because thou art lukewarm, and neither cold nor hot, I will spue thee out of my mouth.**
> Revelation 3:16

That is the standard for who we are as a church. Now there are people who say, "Well, I'm of the church at Philadelphia," and they use it as an arena of superiority. The difference between a member of the church of Laodicea and a member of the church at Philadelphia is very slim. It is not a place of superiority; it is a place of being humble because, except for the grace of God, there go you also. Do not get all exalted in your superior spiritually because you are just dust.

> **For he knoweth our frame; he remembereth that we *are* dust.**
> Psalm 103:14

Revelation 5 is a scene in heaven. The Father is on the throne. They have brought One before Him. In the Father's hand is a book and on the backside it is sealed with seven seals:

> ¹And I saw in the right hand of him that sat on the throne a book written within and on the backside, sealed with seven seals.
>
> ²And I saw a strong angel proclaiming with a loud voice, Who is worthy to open the book, and to loose the seals thereof?
>
> ³And no man in heaven, nor in earth, neither under the earth, was able to open the book, neither to look thereon.

> ⁴And I wept much, because no man was found worthy to open and to read the book, neither to look thereon.
>
> ⁵And one of the elders saith unto me, Weep not: behold, the Lion of the tribe of Juda, the Root of David, hath prevailed to open the book, and to loose the seven seals thereof.
>
> ⁶And I beheld, and, lo, in the midst of the throne and of the four beasts, and in the midst of the elders, stood a Lamb as it had been slain, having seven horns and seven eyes, which are the seven Spirits of God sent forth into all the earth.
>
> ⁷And he came and took the book out of the right hand of him that sat upon the throne.   Revelation 5:1-7

He who sat upon the throne is God, the Father.

This is a picture in heaven because that is where God the Father is. Jesus is in heaven with Him and He is making intercession for you. Now here they are; here is the Father on the throne and here is Jesus the Lamb in heaven with Him. The Father has this book with seven seals. There is no one in heaven or in the earth worthy to approach the Father and take the book.

When you come to the elders, there are 24 of them; 12 represent Old Testament saints and 12 represent New Testament saints. It is very important for you to understand there are 12 representing New Testament saints, because the New Testament saints are there also. You would not have 12 elders representing New Testament saints if there were no saints to represent.

> **And when he had taken the book, the four beasts and four *and* twenty elders fell down before the Lamb, having every one of them harps, and golden vials full of odours, which are the prayers of saints.**
> Revelation 5:8

This scene is in heaven. He came and took the book out of the right hand of Him who sat upon the throne. When he had taken the book, the 4 beasts and 24 elders fell down before the Lamb, having every one of them harps and golden vials full of odors which are the prayers of the saints.

They sung a new song, saying, Thou art worthy to take the book, to open the seals thereof: for you were slain and have redeemed us to our God by thy blood out of every kindred and tongue and people and nation You have made us unto our God kings and priests: and we shall reign on the earth.

> **[9] And they sung a new song, saying, Thou art worthy to take the book, and to open the seals thereof: for thou wast slain, and hast redeemed us to God by thy blood out of every kindred, and tongue, and people, and nation;**
>
> **[10] And hast made us unto our God kings and priests: and we shall reign on the earth.**
>
> Revelation 5:9-10

When this is being said, they are in heaven.

Tribulation Period

Now you can understand Zechariah 14:1-5, the day of the LORD cometh. The LORD cometh and all of His saints come with Him to confront the antichrist in the battle of Armageddon. But you cannot come if you have not gone.

The tribulation period does not begin until the first seal is opened. The revelation of the antichrist is not even known until the first seal is opened. The opening of that seal begins the tribulation period of seven years. The first resurrection occurs before the tribulation because we are in heaven.

Out of every kindred, tongue, and nation that had been redeemed by His blood, we are there represented by the 12 elders of the New Testament period. We are there before the throne with all the Old and New Testament saints. The Lamb is there and in this setting we have the beginning of the forward motion of prophetic timeline just after the first resurrection which will bring world events into play for seven years.

> ¹And I saw when the Lamb opened one of the seals, and I heard, as it were the noise of thunder, one of the four beasts saying, Come and see.
>
> ²And I saw, and behold a white horse: and he that sat on him had a bow; and a crown was given unto him: and he went forth conquering, and to conquer.
> Revelation 6:1-2

He went forth conquering and to conquer the antichrist. The first seal opened is the release of the false messiah into the earth to deceive the Jewish nation.

If the antichrist is just now being revealed and this is the opening of the seven years of dealing with national Israel, then the Old and New Testament church is now in heaven at the judgment seat of Christ. When Christ has judged His own, Old and New Testament, He then passed out the rewards, the positions as to what each will do in service as kings and priests.

> For we must all appear before the judgment seat of Christ; that every one may receive the things *done* in *his* body, according to that he hath done, whether *it be* good or bad. 2 Corinthians 5:10

The Lord has weeded out all the tares. In the New Testament Scriptures it indicates that in the day of the judgment seat of Christ, the Lord Himself will say to many people, "Depart from me; I never knew you." Now you have to understand something very clearly: at the judgment seat of Christ, there will be some believers who make it there, but who are rejected.

But there is justice as to why they are rejected. They say, "Lord, we have healed people in Your name. Lord, we have cast out devils; we have preached the gospel." He says, "Depart from me, ye workers of iniquity, I never knew you."

> [21]Not every one that saith unto me, Lord, Lord, shall enter into the kingdom of heaven; but he that doeth the will of my Father which is in heaven.
>
> [22]Many will say to me in that day, Lord, Lord, have we not prophesied in thy name? and in thy name have cast out devils? and in thy name done many wonderful works?
>
> [23]And then will I profess unto them, I never knew you: depart from me, ye that work iniquity. Matthew 7:21-23

So it is not what *you do* for the Lord. It is who *you are* on the inside as a spiritual being. God does not want to take your works into eternity; He wants to take you. He wants to know what He is getting when He takes you.

If Lucifer could sin, then any created being could also sin. Your heart is being tried right now, right here, this day, in this generation, as to whether He can trust you with mankind. That is why it is important for you to love each other and forgive each other.

If you will not take care of your brother and sister, how can you possibly take care of creation in eternity?

So we have the beginning of the tribulation period, with the identification and the release of the antichrist. Then in Revelation 7:3, an angel comes and seals 144,000 unmarried Jewish men, 12,000 from each tribe except the tribe of Dan.

> **³Saying, Hurt not the earth, neither the sea, nor the trees, till we have sealed the servants of our God in their foreheads.**
>
> **⁴And I heard the number of them which were sealed:** *and there were* **sealed an hundred *and* forty *and* four thousand of all the tribes of the children of Israel.** Revelation 7:3-4

The reason there are none from the tribe of Dan is because the tribe of Dan was the first tribe to go into apostasy, remove the Levites and set up the first occultic Christian church within Judaism.

Many people struggle over who the antichrist is. He is a Jew. He is not the Pope because the Pope is not Jewish. He is a Jew because Daniel said the beast is one who has forsaken the God of His fathers.

> **Neither shall he regard the God of his fathers, nor the desire of women, nor regard any god: for he shall magnify himself above all.** Daniel 11:37

That is a peculiar Jewish idiom which is never used in that way about any other religion or any other group of people on the face of this earth. The antichrist comes from the tribe of Dan because Moses prophesied in Genesis that Dan would judge his brethren.

> **Dan shall judge his people, as one of the tribes of Israel.** Genesis 49:16

At no time in the history of Judaism has the tribe of Dan ever judged his brother. But this time, the tribe of Dan will judge his brother. How does he judge his brother? All of the other tribes follow the false messiah, so Judaism becomes another occultic religion.

Now in the midst of this are those who begin to hear. In the midst of this are angels preaching the gospel from the heavenlies. In the midst of this are the 144,000 unmarried Jewish men who begin to preach the gospel.

In the midst of this there will be the greatest revival ever to hit the nation of Israel, as Jews en masse begin to accept the Messiah. But in the midst of this, a large percentage of the nation will harden their hearts. There will be those who listen and there will be those who do not, just as it is in Gentile nations. There are those who have listened and there are those who have never listened and never will.

In Revelation 5, everyone is in heaven. Revelation 6 is the release of the beginning of the tribulation period. Revelation 7 is the gospel being preached to national Israel. The first 3½ years are 3½ years of peace. This messiah is quite a guy! They are happy; they have their messiah. Revelation 8 begins the splitting of the tribulation period that matches Daniel 12 and then we have angels being dispatched from heaven to match the apostasy.

In Revelation 8:7 we find the first asteroid, or it could be an extreme meteor shower. It could possibly be not just a single large asteroid, but it may be the forerunner of the big one coming because the damage is not quite as extensive.

The First Trumpet

In Revelation 8:7, the first angel sounded; this is the first trumpet. The first angel sounded and there followed hail and fire mingled with blood and they were cast upon the earth and the third part of trees was burnt up and all green grass was burnt up.

> **The first angel sounded, and there followed hail and fire mingled with blood, and they were cast upon the earth: and the third part of trees was burnt up, and all green grass was burnt up.** Revelation 8:7

So in the beginning of the 3½ years, something comes upon the earth. It is a mixture of hail and fire mingled with blood and one-third part of the trees are burnt up.

Do you understand this is saying one-third of all trees on this planet and all the grass are burnt up? Remember this is all happening in this 3½ year period; most of it is right up front in the first year, 1½ years or 2 years of that 3½ years.

There are two occurrences that follow it.

The Second Trumpet

In Revelation 8:8-9, the second angel sounded and as it were a great mountain burning with fire was cast into the sea and the third part of the sea became blood. And the third part of the creatures which were in the sea and had life died, and the third part of the ships that were on these seas was destroyed.

> ⁸And the second angel sounded, and as it were a great mountain burning with fire was cast into the sea: and the third part of the sea became blood;
>
> 9And the third part of the creatures which were in the sea, and had life, died; and the third part of the ships were destroyed.   Revelation 8:8-9

This is not a volcano erupting and falling into the sea. This has to be clearly something huge, a ball of fire coming out of space that hits the seas and one-third of the ocean systems are impacted on this planet. One-third of all sea life is destroyed. One-third of all ships which were on the sea when it happens are destroyed.

These things are happening in areas that are not exactly where Jerusalem is located. When you study prophecy, the antichrist and the Middle East are somehow spared from these catastrophes. On a planet that is 25,000 miles in circumference, 1/3 of that is 8,333.333. If you divide by 2, you have 4,000.

So, to help you understand the impact of this great mountain full of fire that falls into the oceans, it hits an area that impacts a circle around it by 4,000 miles. Now you could take a compass, center on the seas of China and Japan and this mountain of fire could impact a 4,000-mile radius and never touch the Middle East. You could drop something on America or the Atlantic Ocean and it would barely impact the Middle East or maybe not at all. So, if this is the truth, then Israel is maintained unscathed in the middle of this.

The destruction of 1/3 of all ships and 1/3 of all sea life is pretty intense. This is the second catastrophe that hits this planet in that 3½-year period. So it may be another gigantic asteroid that plunges in through our atmosphere and plunks down somewhere in some of our great oceans.

The Third Trumpet

It does not stop there. Revelation 8:10 lists the third catastrophe. The third angel sounded and there fell a great star from heaven.

> [10]And the third angel sounded, and there fell a great star from heaven, burning as it were a lamp, and it fell upon the third part of the rivers, and upon the fountains of waters;
>
> [11]And the name of the star is called Wormwood: and the third part of the waters became wormwood; and many men died of the waters, because they were made bitter. Revelation 8:10-11

You have heard the old saying "falling stars" and now you know they are meteorites. This is not a little meteorite. Meteorites are small pieces of space dust. Asteroids are huge chunks of rock even as large as small islands in space.

As the third angel sounded, there fell a great star from heaven burning as it were a lamp. It fell upon the third part of rivers and upon the fountain of waters. This one hits land. The first one hit where? Oceans. This one hits land. It fell upon the third part of rivers and upon the fountains of waters. The name of the star is called Wormwood. And the third part of the waters became wormwood and many men died of the waters because they were made bitter.

This means the great falling asteroid, or whatever it is, hits the land, pollutes fresh water and turns it poisonous. The men who drink it die because they are poisoned. So, again, 1/3 of mankind is impacted.

With the first one, there is a great burning furnace which burns 1/3 of all trees and all the grass is destroyed. The second one destroys 1/3 of all sea life. The next one lands on land and poisons the waters. This is all happening in that 3½-year period. Could it be the one that is due here February 1, 2019?

So what do you do with things like this in the news? If you do not know what the Bible says, you might say, "Oh, it will never happen." Statistically, the probability of being killed by an asteroid in your lifetime is greater than being killed in an airplane, a hurricane or a tornado. In your generation it is a probability.

Scripturally, it is a certainty. This planet will be hit. It is a certainty. Those who are hiding out, trying to pretend they will be saved will not survive this. Bomb shelters will not survive this. Hiding in the rocks and farming for yourself will not save you from this. No flesh can be saved from this. The only way you can be saved is to make sure you are part of the first resurrection.

Make sure you are part of the first resurrection!

We cannot talk about asteroids without giving the prophetic timeline because it would not be relevant to you. Remember, to be absent from the body is to be present with the Lord. Do not fear about what is coming.

> **We are confident, *I say*, and willing rather to be absent from the body, and to be present with the Lord.**
> 2 Corinthians 5:8

Our faith is this: we are part of that number in Revelation 5, Old and New Testament saints who sit around the throne in that day talking to the Father, saying "The LAMB, He's worthy; He can take the book and open the seals. Papa, He has redeemed us by His blood out of all of our nations. Give it to Him, Papa."

The Fourth Trumpet

When Jesus takes that book in heaven and opens that first seal, the revelation of the antichrist is right here. What follows these three seals? Two asteroids and one heavenly occurrence burn the trees, and then it gets worse. Those are just three angels. Hear what the fourth one says:

> ⁷And when he had opened the fourth seal, I heard the voice of the fourth beast say, Come and see.
>
> ⁸And I looked, and behold a pale horse: and his name that sat on him was Death, and Hell followed with him. And power was given unto them over the fourth part of the earth, to kill with sword, and with hunger, and with death, and with the beasts of the earth.　　　　　　　　　　Revelation 6:7-8

This takes us to the fifth trumpet, the release of tormenting devils from the pit.

The Fifth Trumpet

Revelation 9:1-12 is the fifth angel.

¹And the fifth angel sounded, and I saw a star fall from heaven unto the earth: and to him was given the key of the bottomless pit.

²And he opened the bottomless pit; and there arose a smoke out of the pit, as the smoke of a great furnace; and the sun and the air were darkened by reason of the smoke of the pit.

³And there came out of the smoke locusts upon the earth: and unto them was given power, as the scorpions of the earth have power.

⁴And it was commanded them that they should not hurt the grass of the earth, neither any green thing, neither any tree; but only those men which have not the seal of God in their foreheads.

⁵And to them it was given that they should not kill them, but that they should be tormented five months: and their torment *was* as the torment of a scorpion, when he striketh a man.

⁶And in those days shall men seek death, and shall not find it; and shall desire to die, and death shall flee from them.

⁷And the shapes of the locusts *were* like unto horses prepared unto battle; and on their heads *were* as it were crowns like gold, and their faces *were* as the faces of men.

⁸And they had hair as the hair of women, and their teeth were as *the teeth* of lions.

> ⁹And they had breastplates, as it were breastplates of iron; and the sound of their wings *was* as the sound of chariots of many horses running to battle.
>
> ¹⁰And they had tails like unto scorpions, and there were stings in their tails: and their power *was* to hurt men five months.
>
> ¹¹And they had a king over them, *which is* the angel of the bottomless pit, whose name in the Hebrew tongue *is* Abaddon, but in the Greek tongue hath *his* name Apollyon.
>
> ¹²One woe is past; *and*, behold, there come two woes more hereafter. Revelation 9:1-12

What happens here? The release of tormenting devils from the pit. The men who are left alive on this planet who are rebels against the living God and who have survived two asteroids and the scorching of the planet will be tormented, causing them to wish they could die. They beg to die.

In those days shall men seek death and shall not find it. They shall desire to die and death shall flee from them. They are becoming insane with tormenting devils that plague them and torment them. They beg to die and God will not allow it. If you miss the first resurrection and you survive an asteroid, this is what is coming if you are still here. Oh, it gets worse than that.

THE SIXTH TRUMPET

Then comes the sixth angel in Revelation 9:13-21:

¹³And the sixth angel sounded, and I heard a voice from the four horns of the golden altar which is before God,

¹⁴Saying to the sixth angel which had the trumpet, Loose the four angels which are bound in the great river Euphrates.

¹⁵And the four angels were loosed, which were prepared for an hour, and a day, and a month, and a year, for to slay the third part of men.

¹⁶And the number of the army of the horsemen were two hundred thousand thousand: and I heard the number of them.

¹⁷And thus I saw the horses in the vision, and them that sat on them, having breastplates of fire, and of jacinth, and brimstone: and the heads of the horses were as the heads of lions; and out of their mouths issued fire and smoke and brimstone.

¹⁸By these three was the third part of men killed, by the fire, and by the smoke, and by the brimstone, which issued out of their mouths.

¹⁹For their power is in their mouth, and in their tails: for their tails were like unto serpents, and had heads, and with them they do hurt.

²⁰And the rest of the men which were not killed by these plagues yet repented not of the works of their hands, that they should not worship devils, and idols of gold, and silver, and brass, and stone, and of wood: which neither can see, nor hear, nor walk:

²¹Neither repented they of their murders, nor of their sorceries, nor of their fornication, nor of their thefts.   Revelation 9:13-21

This angel releases hordes of devils and demons of disease and plague and death. It is a fearful thing to fall into the hands of the living God.

> **²⁶For if we sin wilfully after that we have received the knowledge of the truth, there remaineth no more sacrifice for sins,**
>
> **²⁷But a certain fearful looking for of judgment and fiery indignation, which shall devour the adversaries.**
>
> **²⁸He that despised Moses' law died without mercy under two or three witnesses:**
>
> **²⁹Of how much sorer punishment, suppose ye, shall he be thought worthy, who hath trodden under foot the Son of God, and hath counted the blood of the covenant, wherewith he was sanctified, an unholy thing, and hath done despite unto the Spirit of grace?**
>
> **³⁰For we know him that hath said, Vengeance *belongeth* unto me, I will recompense, saith the Lord. And again, The Lord shall judge his people.**
>
> **³¹*It is* a fearful thing to fall into the hands of the living God.** Hebrews 10:26-31

These things must be taught and must be understood by the Christian church so you may be an accurate oracle for what the living God has said about the future. Otherwise, what kind of gospel are you preaching?

Believer, get right with God! Oh, we bring a few gifts called healing of disease and disease prevention, but that is a bonus! That is His mercy; that is His grace so you can be delivered from the consequences of sin while you are here and have a better life.

But the issue is this: The newspaper articles and scientists are concerned this planet will be hit. One-third of it will be scorched; then a huge asteroid shall hit our seas. One-third will hit land and pollute our waters, all in the tribulation period.

THE SEVENTH TRUMPET

The seventh angel sounds in Revelation 11:15-19:

> ¹⁵And the seventh angel sounded; and there were great voices in heaven, saying, The kingdoms of this world are become *the kingdoms* of our Lord, and of his Christ; and he shall reign for ever and ever.
>
> ¹⁶And the four and twenty elders, which sat before God on their seats, fell upon their faces, and worshipped God,
>
> ¹⁷Saying, We give thee thanks, O Lord God Almighty, which art, and wast, and art to come; because thou hast taken to thee thy great power, and hast reigned.
>
> ¹⁸And the nations were angry, and thy wrath is come, and the time of the dead, that they should be judged, and that thou shouldest give reward unto thy servants the prophets, and to the saints, and them that fear thy name, small and great; and shouldest destroy them which destroy the earth.
>
> ¹⁹And the temple of God was opened in heaven, and there was seen in his temple the ark of his testament: and there were lightnings, and voices, and thunderings, and an earthquake, and great hail.
> Revelation 11:15-19

Prayer

Father, thank You for Your Word. Thank You for what the prophet Amos has told us by the Spirit of God: You would do nothing in the earth unless You have first revealed it through Your prophets, that we may fear and understand the totality of mankind's journey.

We have been here almost 6000 years from Adam. There will only be 7000 years in this dispensation of time and we are at the closing hours, even closing minutes, of the sixth day of Your dealing with mankind. Let us be challenged; let us talk about these things in our homes, in the workplace and with strangers. Let us talk about what we think concerning asteroids hitting the earth and if the Bible has anything to say about it and why.

Father, if the scientists are right, an asteroid will hit this planet in 2019. If the scientists see this thing, and they do, and it is on a direct path to hit our planet and it is a huge asteroid, 1½ miles wide, then we are on a collision course with destiny. We are on a collision course, not with an asteroid, but with our destiny as believers.

Father, let our hearts be challenged to stay faithful to You. Let us understand that You have intended this planet be inhabited in righteousness. The issue is not terrorism, necessarily. The issue is not the stock market, necessarily. The issue is this: are we right with God? Will we be part of the first resurrection? Will we be in heaven in Revelation 5, or will we be here, knowing these things are true and shall surely come to pass?

Father, I ask that our hearts be encouraged, be challenged, be strengthened this day in the name of Jesus. Amen.

Bibliography

US News and World Report, January 15, 2001, "Heading Our Way"

Discover, February 2001, "Rendezvous with a Killer Asteroid"

Newsweek, November 23, 1992, "The Science of Doom"

Florida Times-Union, November 20, 1991, "Strange Space Object Heads Towards Earth"

Atlanta Journal-Constitution, February 17, 1997, "The Smoking Gun"

USA Today, December 5, 2000, "Doomsday May Be on the Way: But Don't Brace for a Deep Impact Just Yet"

USA Today, February 23, 2001, "A Comet May Have Triggered Mass Extinction"

National Geographic News, April 9, 2002

Florida Times-Union, July 1, 1991

CNN, July 24, 2002

Reuters News, July 24, 2002

Associated Press, July 24, 2002